SCIENCE FOR THE FUTURE
EXPLORING OCEAN
DEPTHS

by Clara MacCarald

T0014654

FOCUS
READERS

VOYAGER

www.focusreaders.com

Copyright © 2020 by Focus Readers, Lake Elmo, MN 55042. All rights reserved. No part of this book may be reproduced or utilized in any form or by any means without written permission from the publisher.

Focus Readers is distributed by North Star Editions:
sales@northstareditions.com | 888-417-0195

Produced for Focus Readers by Red Line Editorial.

Content Consultant: Kevin Kocot, Assistant Professor, Department of Biological Sciences, University of Alabama

Photographs ©: Jeffrey Rotman/Science Source, cover, 1; Jaime Henry-White/AP Images, 4–5; Red Line Editorial, 7; Neil Bromhall/Shutterstock Images, 8–9; Album/Alamy, 11; Sir John Murray/Voyage To Inner Space - Exploring the Seas With NOAA Collection/NOAA, 13; AP Images, 14–15, 17; Pacific Ring of Fire 2004 Expedition/NOAA Office of Ocean Exploration; Dr. Bob Embley, NOAA PMEL, Chief Scientist/NOAA, 19; NOAA, 20–21; David Burdick/NOAA's Coral Kingdom Collection/NOAA, 22; Gavin Eppard, WHOI/Expedition to the Deep Slope/OER/NOAA, 25; Courtesy of Officers and Crew of NOAA Ship PISCES/Collection of Commander Jeremy Adams/NOAA Corps/NOAA, 26–27; NOS/Office of Coast Survey/NOAA, 28; Mountains in the Sea Research Team/the IFE Crew/OAR/OER/NOAA, 31; Image courtesy of Deepwater Canyons 2013 - Pathways to the Abyss/NOAA-OER/BOEM/USGS, 33; Image courtesy of Expedition to the Deep Slope 2007/NOAA-OE/NOAA, 34–35; stihii/Shutterstock Images, 36; Gregory G. Dimijian/Science Source, 39; Rhonda Roth/Shutterstock Images, 41; Mountains in the Sea 2004/NOAA Office of Ocean Exploration/Dr. Les Watling, Chief Scientist, University of Maine/NOAA, 42–43; Caleb Jones/AP Images, 45

Library of Congress Cataloging-in-Publication Data
Names: MacCarald, Clara, 1979- author.
Title: Exploring ocean depths / by Clara MacCarald.
Description: Lake Elmo, MN : Focus Readers, 2020. | Series: Science for the
   future | Includes bibliographical references and index. | Audience: Grade
   7 to 8.
Identifiers: LCCN 2019008555 (print) | LCCN 2019015496 (ebook) | ISBN
   9781644930038 (pdf) | ISBN 9781641859172 (ebook) | ISBN 9781641857796
   (hardcover) | ISBN 9781641858489 (pbk.)
Subjects: LCSH: Underwater exploration--Juvenile literature.
Classification: LCC GC65 (ebook) | LCC GC65 .M33 2020 (print) | DDC
   551.46072/3--dc23
LC record available at https://lccn.loc.gov/2019008555

Printed in the United States of America
Mankato, MN
May, 2019

ABOUT THE AUTHOR

Clara MacCarald is a freelance writer with a master's degree in biology. She lives with her family in an off-grid house nestled in the forests of central New York. When not parenting her daughter, she spends her time writing nonfiction books for kids.

TABLE OF CONTENTS

CHAPTER 1

A HIDDEN WORLD

In 2012, filmmaker James Cameron squeezed into a lime-green **submersible**. A crane lifted the small vehicle from the deck of a ship and lowered it into the Pacific Ocean. The submersible spun slowly as it began to sink. Far below lay the Mariana Trench. This huge gap in the seafloor contains the deepest points on Earth. The submersible would carry Cameron down to explore the ocean's depths.

A submersible called *Deepsea Challenger* explored the Mariana Trench in 2012.

As the submersible descended, darkness surrounded Cameron. Without the vehicle's lights, he would have seen nothing. And the weight of all the water would have killed him if not for the submersible's thick metal walls.

Finally, Cameron reached the deepest part of the trench. Known as Challenger Deep, it lies 6.8 miles (10.9 km) beneath the ocean's surface. Cameron steered through the barren landscape. Tools on the outside of the submersible collected small creatures and samples of the seafloor.

The deep sea contains amazing ecosystems and valuable resources. In fact, more than 70 percent of Earth's surface lies beneath the ocean. However, very little of the ocean has been explored. Most of the seafloor is dangerous and difficult to reach. Explorers may spend hours or even days underwater. They must bring enough oxygen to last the whole time. They also need protection from crushing pressures and extreme temperatures. Despite these challenges, scientists are working hard on ways to meet them.

GOING DEEP ◀

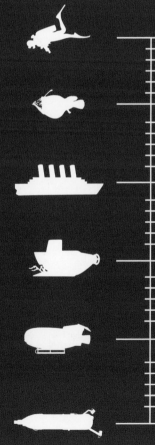

1,090 feet (332 m)
Deepest scuba dive

5,280 feet (1,609 m)
Deepest anglerfish

12,500 feet (3,810 m)
Wreck of the *Titanic*

14,764 feet (4,500 m)
Depth *Alvin* can dive

20,000 feet (6,000 m)
Depth *Mir I* and *Mir II* can dive

35,787 feet (10,908 m)
Cameron's dive to the bottom of Challenger Deep

CHAPTER 2

MYSTERIES BENEATH THE SEA

For much of human history, people could only guess what lay deep below the ocean's surface. Strange creatures occasionally washed up on shore. Storms and rocks sank ancient ships, leaving wrecks hidden underwater. Ancient writers imagined whole cities beneath the sea.

People were determined to explore underwater. The seafloor held sponges and pearls. Divers attempted to reach these valuable resources.

For centuries, people only knew about creatures such as anglerfish from what washed up on shore.

In ancient Greece, sponge divers held heavy rocks to help them sink. Some divers went down nearly 100 feet (30 m) on one breath of air. At that depth, water pressure is approximately four times greater than it is at the surface. The divers may have filled their ears with oil to protect their eardrums from this pressure.

The Greeks and other ancient people wanted to increase the time divers could work underwater. So, they invented diving bells. Diving bells are containers full of air that are held upside down in the water. The air pressure inside keeps water out. The first diving bells may have been pots worn like helmets.

In the 1500s, inventors began improving diving bells. Large bells could hold several people. Some had hoses attached so people could fill them with fresh air pumped from the surface. Still, pressure

▲ This illustration shows a diving bell created by Edmond Halley in the 1600s.

remained a challenge. Air pressure inside the bells increased with depth. High pressure forces a person's body to absorb extra gas. If people return to normal pressure too quickly, the gas forms dangerous bubbles in their tissues and blood. Sometimes divers became sick or even died when they returned to the surface.

As inventors tested divers' limits, people at the surface found other ways to explore. In the 1400s, ocean navigation began to improve. Scientists had a better idea where they were on a map. Still, the deep ocean floor remained a mystery. Scientists guessed that most of it was flat and barren. Many scientists believed nothing could live in the deepest parts of the sea.

In 1872, a group of scientists set sail from England. Their ship, the HMS *Challenger*, had been built for war. But instead of weapons, it now held labs and scientific instruments. The ship's crew sailed around the world on a voyage of discovery.

The scientists studied 362 sites. At each site, they measured the ocean's depth. They also took temperature readings and scooped up samples of the bottom. The scientists found 4,700 new types of organisms, some from the ocean's deepest

areas. The measurements showed that the ocean floor changed a great deal. Towering mountain ranges lay hidden far below the surface. The scientists also discovered the Mariana Trench. They were amazed to find so much life and variety. But these discoveries were only the beginning.

CHAPTER 3

DIVING DEEPER

To travel deeper, people needed protection from pressure. Inventors began to create submersibles. At first, they covered boats in leather or metal to keep out the water. These early submersibles moved using oars or propellers. Some could take on or lose water. The water changed the submersible's weight, making it sink or float. Some of the boats stored compressed air.

Inventor John Philip Holland climbs into an early submersible in 1897.

The air could be released, giving the crew oxygen to breathe.

William Beebe and Otis Barton invented a submersible called the bathysphere. It looked like a steel ball with thick windows. The bathysphere was 4 feet (1.2 m) wide. Cables connected it to a ship. An electric cable provided power, and a telephone cable allowed the crew to talk with people at the surface.

Beebe and Barton first rode in the bathysphere in 1930. They went much deeper than unprotected divers could go. Their first dive reached 803 feet (245 m) below the surface. The men observed deep-sea creatures and the geology of the seafloor. Before going deeper, they tried a test dive. They lowered the bathysphere without a crew. During this test, a leak caused water to fill the craft. The pressure alone would have killed

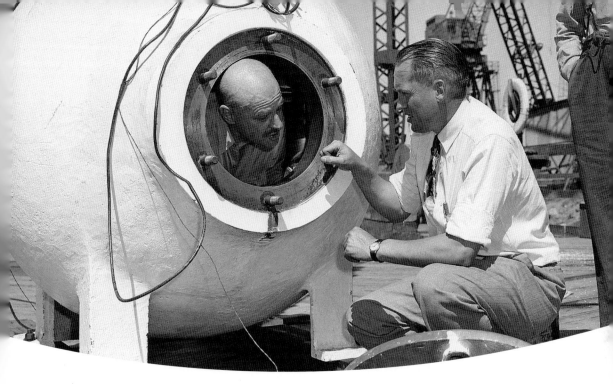

⚓ Otis Barton prepares for a dive in the bathysphere in 1949.

anyone inside. But the danger didn't keep Beebe and Barton from continuing their work.

In 1934, Beebe and Barton used the bathysphere in a part of the ocean near Bermuda. They descended 3,028 feet (923 m). A small window revealed a dark world never before seen by humans. Fish had lights along their sides that flashed like fireflies.

Scientists continued to make deeper dives. In 1960, people first ventured into the Challenger Deep. Their submersible looked like a hot-air balloon made of metal. The top part held **floats**. Beneath it, two people huddled in a cabin just 7 feet (2.1 m) wide. The submersible could take on water to sink. When the submersible reached the seafloor, the scientists were amazed to see a sea cucumber swimming past. Scientists hadn't known animals could survive so far underwater.

In 1977, scientists found animals around a hydrothermal vent. These vents are formed by

> ➤ **THINK ABOUT IT**
>
> If something had gone wrong with the bathysphere, Beebe and Barton could have died. Why do you think some people are willing to risk their lives to explore the ocean's depths?

▲ Mussels, crabs, and other creatures live near the Champagne Vent.

underwater volcanoes. Cracks in the seafloor allow extreme heat and chemicals from deep within the planet to flow into the ocean. Sunlight does not reach these areas, so plants cannot grow. Instead, food webs are based on bacteria.

The bacteria use chemicals for energy. They produce food with this energy, using a process similar to the one plants use to create food from sunlight. Clams, crabs, and other animals can live in extreme conditions thanks to these bacteria.

CHAPTER 4

UNDERWATER OBSERVATION

In the early 1900s, deep-sea divers were still tied to the surface. They wore helmets that received air through tubes. The divers could only go as far as the tubes could reach. To go deeper, divers needed to carry their own air supplies.

In 1878, divers had begun carrying tanks of compressed air. But this gear was dangerous, and divers were limited to shallow water. In 1943, two French inventors created a new kind of air tank.

A diver wears a thick suit to explore a shipwreck in 1935.

▲ Scuba divers swim near the Mariana Islands.

This tank was much safer to use. It also allowed divers to go deeper than ever before. **Scuba diving** soon became popular.

Pressure remained a deadly threat. Divers who go deep must return slowly to normal pressure. This allows the gas to release from their bodies without forming bubbles. The deeper divers go, the slower they must surface. To stay safe, they might need to wait hours before diving again. That way, all the gas has a chance to leave. People can take four days to fully recover after a dive to 300 feet (91 m).

Divers knew they could stay down longer if they had an undersea lab. People built the first undersea lab in 1962. The air inside the lab was the same pressure as the water outside it. As a result, divers could enter and exit the lab quickly without worrying about gas bubbles. In 1964, the US Navy placed Sealab I near Bermuda. Sealab I sat 192 feet (59 m) under the surface. Researchers could spend up to a month living inside. They could dive for several hours each day.

As of 2019, only one undersea lab remains in use. The lab, Aquarius, is off the coast of Florida.

Aquarius rests on sand 62 feet (19 m) below the surface. It sits at the edge of one of the largest coral barrier reefs in the world. Scientists use the lab to monitor ocean conditions, study underwater **ecology**, and test deep-sea equipment.

Submersibles are still the only way to reach most of the seafloor. Modern submersibles come in different shapes and sizes. Their design determines what they can do. Some hold a few people. Others hold only one. Some submersibles get power from batteries. They can operate for hours or even days.

Modern submersibles regularly dive 14,764 feet (4,500 m) below the surface. That's far too deep for the crew to exit the submersible. Instead, the vehicle's robotic arms perform many tasks. For example, these arms can take samples of sediment, rock, and organisms. Submersibles also

▲ *Alvin* first hit the water in 1964. Since then, it has gone through several upgrades.

have lights, cameras, and tools such as **sonar** and lasers.

A submersible called *Alvin* has made more than 4,000 dives. On a typical mission, three people squeeze inside. *Mir I* and *Mir II* are two other submersibles. They can dive approximately 3.7 miles (6.0 km) below the surface. They can reach approximately 98 percent of the ocean floor.

CHAPTER 5

ROBOT SCOUTS

The ocean is vast. Even in submersibles, scientists cannot visit every part. Instead, they use other methods to study the ocean. Some scientists study the ocean from onshore labs. Others work on boats.

Many scientists use sonar. Using this system, they are able to determine how far away an object is. To do so, they send out a sound and time how long it takes for the echo to return.

Scientists use robotic vehicles to study the underwater world.

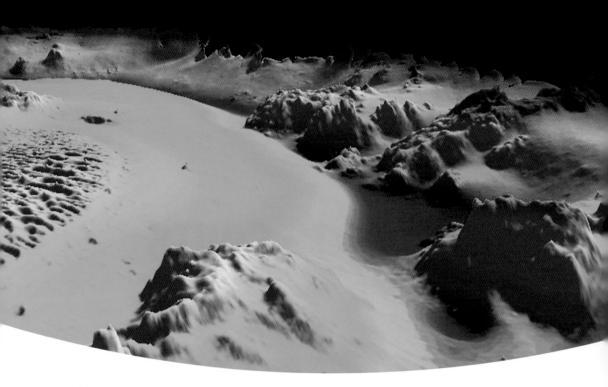

▲ Scientists use sonar to make maps of the ocean floor's features.

Modern sonar can detect extremely small changes miles below the surface.

However, to measure a region's features, a ship must go there. Therefore, sonar may not be the best option in remote areas. Instead, **satellites** can study the ocean from above. They can measure changes in the height of the ocean's water. The changes give clues to features on the seafloor. Huge mountains or trenches make dips or bulges on the surface. But satellites don't give as detailed a picture as sonar can. And submersibles still provide the most detail.

For deep or dangerous dives, scientists may use robotic submersibles. These vehicles do not carry a crew. Instead, scientists control them from a distance. Robots allow scientists to explore the depths with less risk. But using robots has downsides. For instance, people can spot animals more easily than robots can. People may also navigate more carefully in tricky conditions.

A remotely operated vehicle (ROV) is a submersible linked to the surface by cables. Researchers use the cables to control the submersible. The cables also provide the ROV with a constant supply of power. This allows the ROV to operate for long periods of time.

ROVs carry a variety of useful instruments. They often have lights, cameras, arms, sampling tools, sonar, and more. Unfortunately, ROVs cost a lot to make. They can also be difficult to transport out to sea because they are so big. Smaller submersibles with no tie to the surface are cheaper and easier to use. Sometimes these smaller submersibles are called drones.

Drones in the air are controlled by radio signals. However, radio signals can't penetrate very far underwater. If deep-sea drones do communicate with the surface, they use sound. Otherwise they must act on their own. Scientists

➤ THINK ABOUT IT

What are some advantages of programming a drone before its mission? What challenges could this process create?

▲ The ROV *Hercules* explores the seafloor.

program an underwater drone with the commands necessary to carry out its mission. Some drones are programmed to make some of their own decisions. They can change their path or actions based on the conditions they encounter. Drones can travel farther and work longer than ROVs, but they have fewer instruments. Inventors are hard at work designing new drones.

AMANDA DEMOPOULOS

Dr. Amanda Demopoulos is an ecologist. She works for the US Geological Survey (USGS). Her love for the ocean began when she was a child. She wanted to find a career related to the ocean.

In college, Demopoulos became interested in tiny **invertebrates** that live in water. She completed a doctorate in **oceanography** in 2004. Now, Demopoulos studies invertebrates for her job with the USGS. She works with invertebrates that live on the seafloor or in wetlands along the coast.

Sometimes Demopoulos rides submersibles or controls ROVs. She takes samples of organisms to study. Other times she works with material other scientists have scooped up from the bottom. She studies which invertebrates live where and how

▲ Amanda Demopoulos (right) and other scientists examine sediment collected by an ROV.

they interact with one another. She also examines how they respond to challenges such as climate change.

Though small, invertebrates play a large role in marine food webs. Some, such as snails and flatworms, live in mud. They eat organic matter that floats down from water closer to the surface. Some, such as deep-sea coral, filter food from the water. The invertebrates are eaten by larger animals such as fish and crabs.

CHAPTER 6

OCEAN SECRETS

Today, scientists know far more about what the ocean holds than they did a hundred years ago. Many ocean features are formed due to the action of tectonic plates. These huge pieces of Earth's crust are slowly shifting. In some places, they smash into one another. They lift up vast ridges from the ocean floor. In other places, one plate slips underneath another. This process creates the deep trenches.

These tube worms live in a crack in the seafloor in the Gulf of Mexico.

The seafloor contains many unique ecosystems. Near coastlines, relatively shallow areas known as continental shelves teem with life. Beyond them, dark plains stretch deep underwater. The plains have very little food.

➤ FEATURES OF THE OCEAN FLOOR

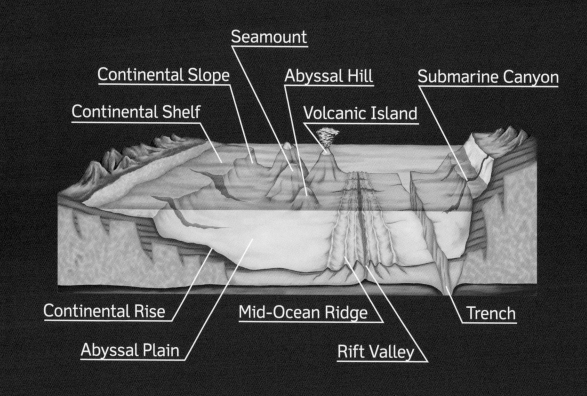

Seamount

Continental Slope   Abyssal Hill   Submarine Canyon

Continental Shelf   Volcanic Island

Continental Rise   Mid-Ocean Ridge   Trench

Abyssal Plain   Rift Valley

Sunlight doesn't reach the deep ocean, so plants and algae can't grow.

Creatures on these plains rely on food from the surface. Dead organisms and animal waste drift down from far above. Fish, sea urchins, and **microorganisms** graze on this material. Sometimes algae populations grow rapidly on the surface. They create clouds of organic matter that float down for deep-sea organisms to consume.

Farther underwater, animals have different food sources. Near hydrothermal vents, food webs are based on chemicals. Chemicals also leak out of the ground at cold seeps. These cracks in the seafloor support many kinds of life. Bacteria near cold seeps use the chemicals to produce energy. Animals near seeps grow much more slowly than those near hot vents. But they tend to live longer. Tube worms at seeps may live up to 250 years.

Deep-sea creatures have adapted other tricks for survival. One is bioluminescence, or the ability to give off light. Many ocean animals use light to escape predators, attract mates, and find food. Some squids squirt out clouds of blinding light. The light surprises predators so the squid can swim away. An anglerfish uses light to attract food. This creature has a fishing rod built into its head. A small piece of bioluminescent flesh wriggles at the end. Other fish think the light is a meal. When they swim toward it, the anglerfish eats them.

Studying the ocean floor also helps scientists learn about human history. As many as three million ships and planes may lie on the bottom. These wrecks reveal things about the people who built them. For example, the Mediterranean Sea holds ships from ancient Greece and Rome.

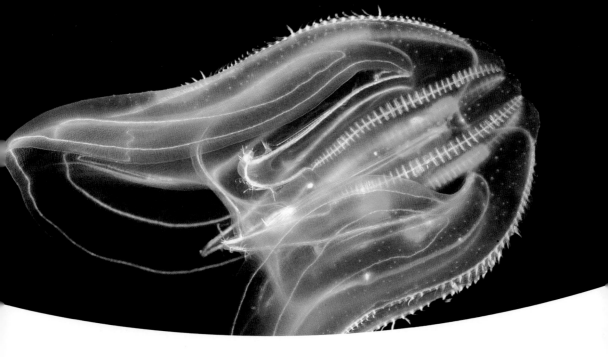

▲ Some jellyfish produce light to scare predators.

Studying their locations and cargo helps people learn about trade in ancient times.

In 1985, researchers found the wreck of the RMS *Titanic*. This enormous ship crashed into an iceberg in 1912. By exploring the wreck, researchers learned details about how the ship sank. They discovered that the *Titanic* broke apart and slipped quickly underwater. Many other ocean secrets lie in the depths, waiting to be discovered.

LIHINI ALUWIHARE

Dr. Lihini Aluwihare is a professor at the Scripps Institution of Oceanography. Born in Sri Lanka, Aluwihare also lived in Zambia and England when she was young. She went to college in Massachusetts to study chemistry. One summer, she helped out at the Woods Hole Oceanographic Institution. Aluwihare realized the field of marine chemistry offered the promise of adventure.

After graduating, Aluwihare became a professor at the University of California. Now she runs a lab at Scripps. There, she performs research. She also guides students through their own projects.

Aluwihare focuses on how microorganisms and chemicals interact in the ocean. One important chemical element she studies is carbon. Carbon in the atmosphere affects Earth's climate. Enormous amounts of carbon occur in the ocean. Scientists

△ The Scripps Institution of Oceanography uses a long pier to study conditions in the ocean.

don't fully understand where the carbon came from or where it's going. But they do know that microorganisms play a big role in recycling the carbon from organic matter. Aluwihare's research aims to better understand the processes involved.

Part of Aluwihare's work involves heading out to sea. She goes on cruises to take samples and measurements. She works with delicate instruments out on the water. Aluwihare enjoys the challenges and variety the job brings.

CHAPTER 7

A BLUE FUTURE

Some human actions damage the ocean depths. Deep-sea fishing harms the seafloor and hurts fish populations. Deep-sea mining could destroy ecosystems and pollute large areas. Trash and pollution can poison or kill sea creatures.

In 2018, scientists reported on the problem of human-made garbage in the ocean. They looked at photos and videos collected on 5,010 dives over 30 years. They found 3,425 pieces of trash.

Scientists study corals and other animals that live on the seafloor.

Most of the plastic was the kind people used just once before throwing away. Scientists even spotted a plastic bag in the Mariana Trench. It was nearly 36,000 feet (10,970 m) below the surface.

Because of these threats, scientists are racing against time. They're trying to understand the deep-sea world before large parts are destroyed or greatly altered. From 2000 to 2010, more than 2,700 scientists worked on the **Census** of Marine Life. They examined historical records and performed new research. They learned about known species and discovered more than 1,200 new ones.

> ## ➤ THINK ABOUT IT

What are the advantages of combining data from several studies?

▲ In 2016, scientists took samples of deep-sea coral from an underwater volcano near Hawaii.

Seabed 2030 is a project that aims to map the entire ocean floor. First, scientists will gather all the depth maps people have already created. They will see where information is missing. Then they can target those areas for future mapping.

Scientists continue to share their work with the public. By teaching others about the incredible ecosystems that exist deep below the surface, scientists can gain support for their efforts to protect this amazing part of Earth.

FOCUS ON
EXPLORING
OCEAN DEPTHS

Write your answers on a separate piece of paper.

1. Write a paragraph describing one of the challenges of deep-sea exploration and a solution scientists created to meet it.

2. If you were a scientist, would you rather work in an onshore lab or travel underwater in a submersible? Why?

3. What is the name of the deepest point in the ocean?

     A. Aquarius

     B. Bermuda

     C. Challenger Deep

4. Why were scientists surprised to find animals living near deep-sea hydrothermal vents?

     A. The lack of sunlight means there are no plants to eat.

     B. Undersea fishing is very common in these areas.

     C. These areas are too hot to support life.

Answer key on page 48.

GLOSSARY

census
A count of an area's population.

ecology
The relationship of living things to one another and their surroundings.

floats
Devices that rise in water.

invertebrates
Animals that do not have backbones.

microorganisms
Tiny creatures, such as bacteria, that can be seen only with microscopes.

oceanography
The study of the ocean and the life-forms that live there.

satellites
Objects or vehicles that orbit a planet or moon, often to collect information.

scuba diving
A method of swimming that involves breathing through a mask that is connected to an air tank worn on the back.

sonar
A system for measuring distances and finding objects underwater by sending sound pulses.

submersible
A vehicle designed to operate under the water.

TO LEARN MORE

BOOKS

Burgan, Michael. *Finding the Titanic: How Images from the Ocean Depths Fueled Interest in the Doomed Ship.* North Mankato, MN: Compass Point Books, 2018.

Hand, Carol. *Bringing Back Our Oceans.* Minneapolis: Abdo Publishing, 2018.

Swanson, Jennifer. *Astronaut, Aquanaut.* Washington, DC: National Geographic, 2018.

NOTE TO EDUCATORS

Visit **www.focusreaders.com** to find lesson plans, activities, links, and other resources related to this title.

INDEX

Answer Key: 1. Answers will vary; 2. Answers will vary; 3. C; 4. A